TURI

Travel Guide 2024

A Comprehensive Travel Guide to Exploring Landscapes, Scenic Beauty, Rich Heritage, Hidden Gems, and Cultural Wonders, Alongside Insider Tips for a Memorable Vacation

STANLEY P. THAYER

Copyright ©Stanley P. Thayer, 2024.

All rights reserved. No part of this publication may be reproduced, distributed, or transmitted in any form or by any means, including photocopying, recording, or other electronic or mechanical methods, without the prior written permission of the publisher, except in the case of brief quotations embodied in critical reviews and certain other non-commercial uses permitted by copyright law.

Table of Contents

INTRODUCTION

    Welcome to Turkey

    Brief Overview of Turkey

    Travel Tips and Cultural Etiquette

PLANNING YOUR TRIP

    Best Time to Visit

    Visa Requirements

    Currency and Money Matters

    Language and Communication

GETTING THERE

    Airports and Airlines

    Land and Sea Transportation

ACCOMMODATION

    Types of Accommodation

    Popular Accommodation Areas

DESTINATIONS

   Istanbul

   Cappadocia

   Pamukkale

ACTIVITIES IN TURKEY

   Cultural Experiences

   Outdoor Adventures

FOOD AND DINING IN TURKEY

   Turkish Cuisine

   Dining Etiquette and Customs

   Recommended Restaurants by Region

SHOPPING IN TURKEY

   Traditional Souvenirs

      Grand Bazaars and Markets

      Modern Shopping Districts

HEALTH AND SAFETY

    Travel Insurance

    Health Precautions and Vaccinations

    Emergency Services and Hospitals

CULTURAL INSIGHTS

    Religion and Customs

    Art and Architecture

    Festivals and Celebrations

PRACTICAL INFORMATION

    Local Transportation

    Communication and Internet

    Tipping and Bargaining Tips

SUSTAINABLE TRAVEL

    Responsible Tourism Practices

    Eco-Friendly Accommodation

    Community Engagement Opportunities

RESOURCES

    Useful Websites and Apps

Recommended Reading

Maps and Navigation Tools

CONCLUSION

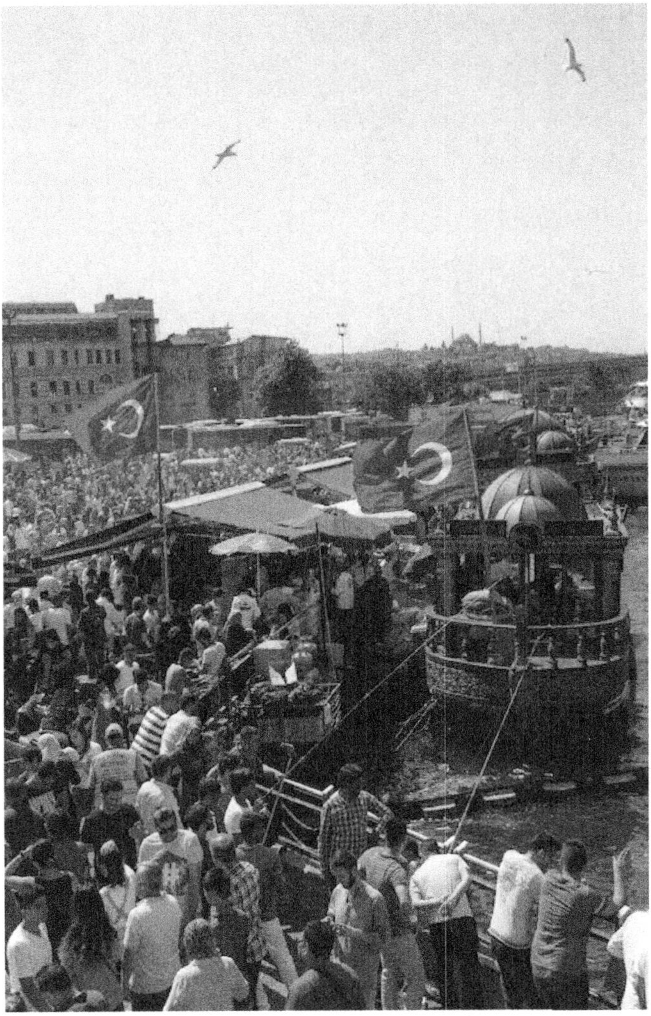

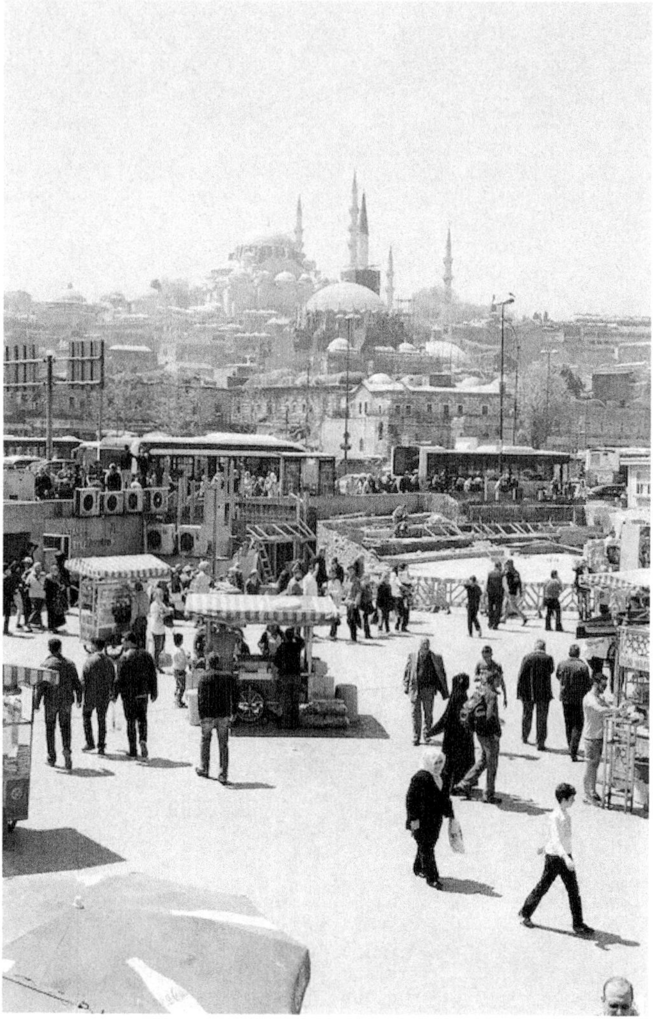

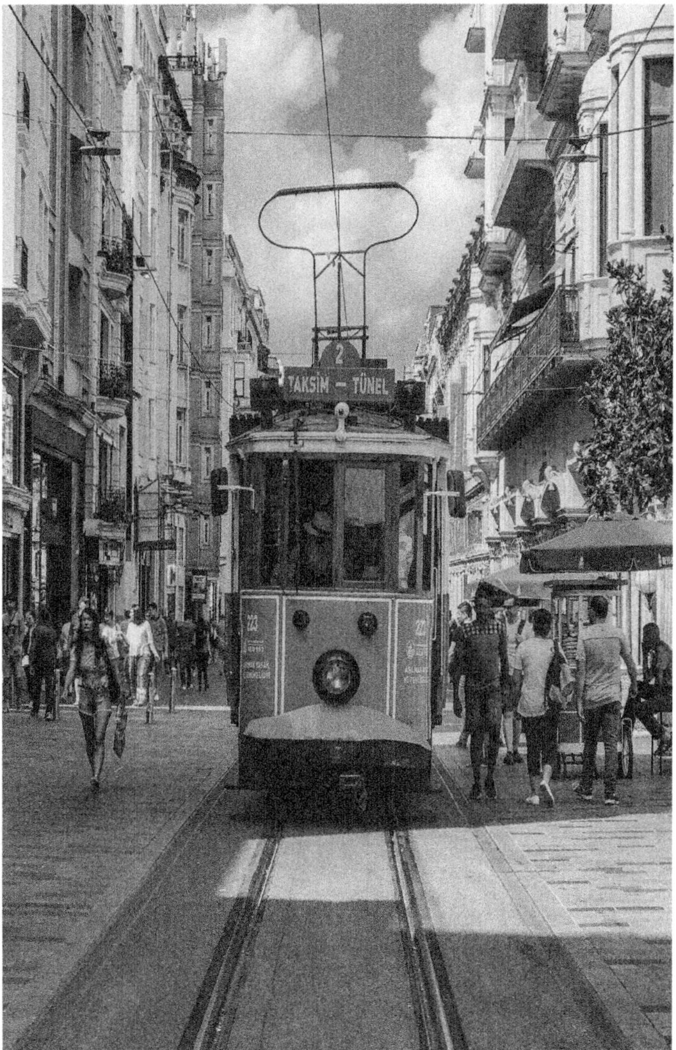
2
TAKSIM – TÜNEL

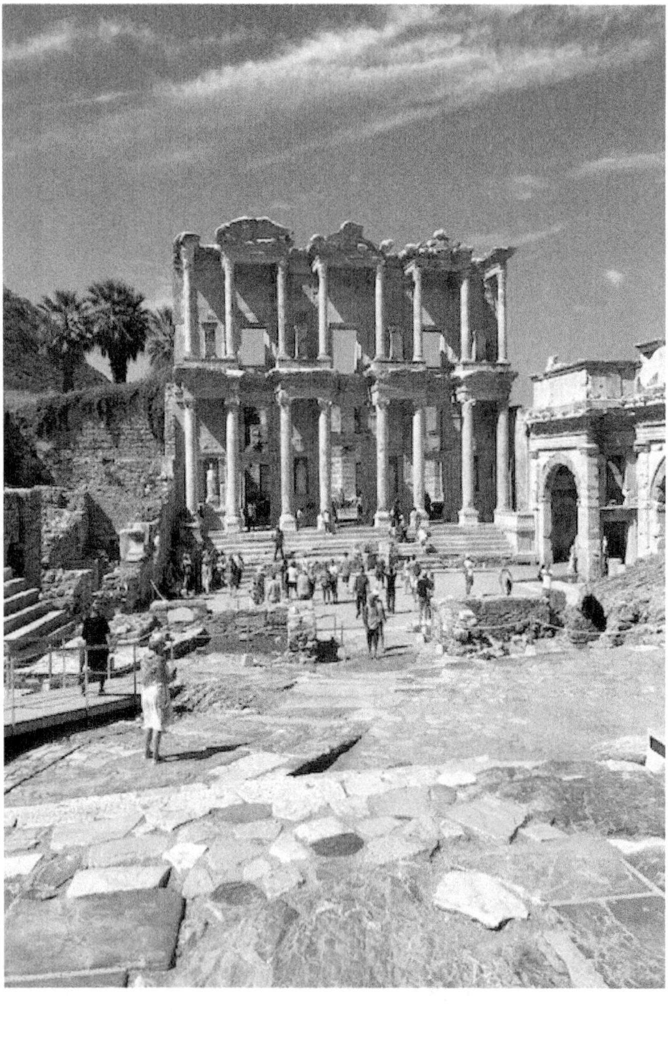

INTRODUCTION

Welcome to Turkey

Welcome to Turkey, a location that encompasses continents and civilizations, presenting an unparalleled blend of ancient history, colorful traditions, and breathtaking beauty. As you stroll onto this unique crossroads between Europe and Asia, you'll find yourself immersed in a tapestry of sensations that run from the crowded markets of Istanbul to the odd panoramas of Cappadocia.

Turkey extends a warm welcome to travelers, urging them to explore its rich history, revel in its diverse cuisine, and see the seamless marriage of the old and the present. From the minute you arrive, you'll be charmed by the warmth of the Turkish people, known for their friendliness and genuine generosity. Prepare to be charmed by a place that masterfully combines the relics of bygone civilizations with the brightness of current life.

Brief Overview of Turkey

Spanning over two centuries, Turkey has a history that dates back to ancient times, with influences from the Hittites, Phrygians, Urartians, and more. Its historical significance is proven by major sites such as the Hagia Sophia, the Blue Mosque, and the ancient city of Troy. Beyond its historical treasures, Turkey's variegated topography contains stunning beaches along the Mediterranean and Aegean coastlines, unusual panoramas in Cappadocia, and the majestic peaks of the Taurus Mountains.

Modern Turkey is a lively blend of East and West, with cosmopolitan cities like Istanbul providing a contrast of historic architecture and modern art scenes. From the bustling street markets to the tranquil olive groves, every corner of Turkey has a narrative to tell. Discover the country's cultural tapestry via its festivals, art, and culinary delights, where the flavors of kebabs, baklava, and Turkish delights will tickle your taste buds.

Travel Tips and Cultural Etiquette

Before going on your Turkish vacation, it's necessary to educate yourself on specific travel norms and cultural etiquette to ensure a comfortable and respectful journey. Turks are famous for their kindness, and learning their customs might enhance your experience.

In terms of apparel, while Turkey is modern and international, it's vital to dress modestly, especially when visiting holy institutions. When entering someone's home, remember to remove your shoes as a mark of respect. Bargaining is a regular activity in markets; therefore, don't hesitate to join in friendly bargaining.

Turkish cuisine is a feature of each visit, with inhabitants taking pride in their traditional delicacies. Remember to taste local cuisine and revel in the ritual of Turkish tea or coffee. Learning a few basic phrases in Turkish, such as greetings and expressions of appreciation, would be appreciated by the locals.

Being aware of cultural nuances, such as the significance of religious holidays, may help you manage social situations with grace. Turks cherish personal relationships, so don't be alarmed if chats extend beyond standard niceties. Embrace the real warmth of the Turkish people and your journey around this intriguing country will be a fantastic experience.

PLANNING YOUR TRIP

Embarking on a vacation to Turkey needs rigorous planning to guarantee you make the most of your trip in this culturally rich and geographically diversified country. From deciding the perfect time to trip to grasping crucial practicalities, this section will lead you through the main components of preparing a superb holiday to Turkey.

Best Time to Visit

Determining the optimum time to visit Turkey is vital to designing an itinerary that matches your tastes and interests. The land enjoys varied seasons, each having its attraction.

Weather and Climate

Turkey's climate varies from the coastal portions to the inland areas. The coastal regions, including Istanbul, have a Mediterranean climate with hot, dry summers and temperate, wet winters. Inland locations, such as Cappadocia, see more extreme weather, with hot summers and frigid winters.

Spring (April to June) and autumn (September to November) are often rated as the ideal seasons to visit. During these seasons, temperatures are pleasant, and the landscapes come alive with blossoming flowers or autumn hues. Summer (June to August) is wonderful for beach places, while winter (December to February) sends tourists to ski resorts in the alpine zones.

Festivals and Events

Turkey hosts a myriad of festivals and events throughout the year, offering a unique insight into its cultural fabric. The Istanbul Music Festival in June, the International Antalya Film Festival in October, and the Mevlana Whirling Dervishes Festival in December are just a few examples. Incorporating these activities into your travel plans may improve your cultural experience and help you develop a better connection with the local traditions.

Visa Requirements

Understanding Turkey's visa requirements is crucial before your vacation begins. While residents of some countries may enter visa-free for short durations, others need to get a visa in advance. The e-Visa system allows many travelers to apply online, speeding the process. Ensure that you check the applicable requirements based on your nationality and the purpose of your visit.

Currency and Money Matters

Turkey's official currency is the Turkish Lira (TRY). It's advisable to convert currencies at banks or official exchange offices for the best rates. Credit cards are usually accepted in urban locations, yet maintaining additional cash is advisable, especially in more distant situations. ATMs are routinely available, giving convenient access to local currency.

Language and Communication

Turkish is the official language of Turkey, yet English is often used in tourist zones and big cities. Learning a few simple Turkish phrases, however, is always appreciated and may increase your contacts with locals. Embrace the possibility of conversing in the local language, developing a greater connection with the culture and people you encounter during your travels.

In the comprehensive preparation phase, identifying the ideal time to visit, handling visa processes, managing cash, and mastering the local language are essential milestones. By addressing these areas, you set the groundwork for a seamless and happy exploration of Turkey's attractions.

GETTING THERE

Navigating the logistics of coming to Turkey is a vital step in having a flawless and joyful vacation experience. Whether arriving by air, land, or sea, understanding the transit possibilities and primary gates is crucial for a seamless entrance into this unique country.

Airports and Airlines

Turkey boasts a well-developed network of airports, connecting major cities and regions.

Istanbul Airport

As the primary international gateway, Istanbul Airport stands as a symbol of modernity and efficiency. Located on the European side of Istanbul, it is one of the largest airports in the world. The site boasts state-of-the-art amenities, various shopping alternatives, and a range of dining choices. Istanbul Airport operates as an important hub for Turkish Airlines, giving extensive access to cities globally.

Ankara Esenboğa Airport

Ankara Esenboğa Airport serves as the capital's primary aviation hub. While not as vast as Istanbul Airport, Esenboğa has a range of local and limited international flights. The airport is well-equipped with amenities catering to both pleasure and business tourists, making it a useful entrance point for those having Ankara as their primary aim.

Other Major Airports

Beyond Istanbul and Ankara, several additional airports give admission into diverse locations of Turkey. Antalya Airport, located on the Mediterranean coast, is a popular location for vacationers traveling to the southern resorts. Izmir Adnan Menderes Airport serves the western coast, enabling access to historic sights like Ephesus. Each major airport contributes to the accessibility and simplicity of traveling within Turkey.

Land and Sea Transportation

Buses and Domestic Transportation

Turkey's large bus network offers a cost-effective and efficient approach to visiting the country. Inter-city buses connect large urban regions, delivering comfortable and reliable travel. Bus companies provide many degrees of service, from plain to luxurious, according to varied passenger preferences. The well-maintained road infrastructure offers comfortable rides, with buses often equipped with conveniences such as Wi-Fi and refreshments.

For those wanting a more independent experience, leasing a car gives them flexibility in discovering Turkey's varied landscapes. The road system is well-developed, enabling visitors to embark on road adventures across gorgeous highways, uncovering hidden pearls along the way.

Ferries and Boats

Turkey's unique geographical condition, flanked by seas on three sides, makes marine transportation an intriguing possibility. Istanbul, with its iconic Bosphorus Strait, has regular ferry services between the European and Asian sides of the city.

Additionally, coastal cities like Izmir and Bodrum have well-established ferry connections to adjacent islands, offering possibilities for island-hopping excursions.

For a leisurely trip and a new perspective of the coastline, tourists may also enjoy boat excursions in the Aegean and Mediterranean seas. These cruises give a pleasant method to observe the coastal grandeur, stopping at areas of historical importance and active local culture.

In summary, going to Turkey involves a well-connected air network via major airports, a solid bus system for interior travel, and gorgeous maritime links for those preferring nautical activities. Understanding these transportation possibilities ensures a successful arrival and sets the tone for your tour of Turkey's different landscapes and cultural resources.

ACCOMMODATION

Choosing the correct hotel is a vital component of any travel experience, determining the comfort and environment of your stay. In Turkey, a country rich in history and various landscapes, accommodations range from great hotels to unique stays, each giving a special sense of Turkish hospitality.

Types of Accommodation

Hotels

Turkey has a huge selection of motels catering to diverse interests and inclinations. In huge cities like Istanbul, Ankara, and Izmir, you'll encounter globally recognized businesses offering premium amenities and stunning views. These hotels often mix modern conveniences with a tinge of Turkish elegance, delivering pleasant relaxation after a day of travel.

For those seeking cultural immersion, boutique hotels in historical areas provide a more intimate experience. These firms usually occupy reconstructed Ottoman-era buildings, retaining the grandeur of the past while delivering customized service. Turkey's hotels, regardless of grade, take pride in warm hospitality, making travelers feel welcome throughout their stay.

Boutique Guesthouses

Boutique guesthouses offer an alternative to the larger hotel experience, giving a more tailored and geographically immersing stay.

Nestled in lovely places, these guesthouses typically reflect the distinctive character of their surroundings. Proprietors, keen about sharing their culture, may give insider suggestions on hidden treasures, building a sense of kinship among tourists.

These guesthouses, with few rooms, emphasize offering a home away from home atmosphere. You may find individual details like handcrafted breakfasts with local delicacies and communal locations that stimulate communication among visitors. Staying at a boutique guesthouse allows you to connect with the local people and receive insights into the authentic Turkish way of life.

Unique Stays

Turkey presents several eccentric and fascinating hotel choices, adding an extra depth of fun to your vacation. In Cappadocia, cave hotels built into the region's remarkable rock formations provide an unmatched experience. Sleeping in a subterranean room adorned with traditional Turkish décor while enjoying modern amenities is an experience in itself.

Treehouses, particularly in seaside regions like Olympos, provide a whimsical holiday surrounded by nature. Nestled between woods, these eco-friendly hotels mix sustainability with comfort. Waking up to the sounds of nature and potentially eating a cooked breakfast on your treehouse terrace creates great memories.

Popular Accommodation Areas

Istanbul

Istanbul, a city straddling two continents, presents a broad array of housing possibilities. The old Sultanahmet neighborhood, home to famous monuments like the Hagia Sophia and Blue Mosque, is studded with modest boutique hotels. Taksim Square and Beyoglu attract travelers desiring a lively setting with fashionable hotels and proximity to Istanbul's famed nightlife.

Cappadocia

Cappadocia's amazing landscapes are matched by equally unusual hotels. Cave hotels and boutique guesthouses in regions like Göreme provide an immersive experience amid fairy chimneys and ancient rock formations. Some restaurants even give hot air balloon views directly from their terraces.

Coastal Resorts

Turkey's spectacular coastal areas, particularly Bodrum, Antalya, and Fethiye, are famous for their luxury resorts. These resorts, often situated along magnificent beaches, provide all-inclusive packages, spa services, and a tranquil respite from the busy city life. Coastal hotels provide a terrific blend of relaxation and fun.

Choosing the finest accommodation in Turkey entails considering your preferences, whether it's the grandeur of a city hotel, the charm of a boutique guesthouse, or the uniqueness of a cave home. Whatever your option, Turkish hospitality ensures a comfortable and delightful stay, adding to the overall depth of your vacation experience.

DESTINATIONS

Turkey, a nation rich in history and ornamented with various landscapes, urges travelers to experience its amazing sites. From the frenetic metropolis of Istanbul to the bizarre landscapes of Cappadocia and the natural wonders of Pamukkale, each destination delivers a different tapestry of experiences, mixing cultural richness with natural beauty.

Istanbul

As Turkey's cultural and economic hub, Istanbul is a city where the old easily intertwines with the new. This dynamic metropolis, straddling the continents of Europe and Asia, offers a treasure trove of experiences.

Top Attractions

Istanbul's skyline is studded with iconic landmarks that communicate tales of its rich past. The Hagia Sophia, once a church and subsequently a mosque, presently exists as a museum, showcasing Byzantine and Ottoman architectural masterpieces. The Blue Mosque, with its stunning tilework and towering minarets, elicits awe and contemplation. The Grand Bazaar, a tangle of active kiosks, is a sensory feast with its vibrant colors, smells, and noises.

Cultural and Historical Sites

Delve into Istanbul's history by seeing the Topkapi Palace, a former royal home boasting imperial artifacts and stunning gardens. The Basilica Cistern, an underground reservoir with ancient columns and reflections on water, gives a magical experience. The Archaeological Museum and Istanbul Modern Art Museum provide perspectives into Turkey's artistic and historical past.

Dining and Nightlife

Istanbul's culinary scene is a blend of flavors reflecting its multicultural background. Indulge in a gastronomic adventure at the Spice Bazaar and enjoy Turkish favorites, baklava, and kebabs. The city's nightlife comes alive in areas like Beyoglu and Kadikoy, where rooftop bars, traditional meyhanes, and live music venues create a vibrant setting for nocturnal exploration.

Cappadocia

Cappadocia, a captivating place in central Turkey, is known for its surreal landscapes formed by wind and time. This site offers a strange voyage and a glimpse into the region's particular past.

Fairy Chimneys and Rock Formations

The fairy chimneys of Cappadocia are natural wonders, towering cone-shaped rock formations produced by volcanic activity.

Goreme National Park and the Rock Sites of Cappadocia, a UNESCO World Heritage Site, emphasize these extraordinary geological formations, providing a bizarre atmosphere that looks almost extraterrestrial.

Hot Air Balloon Rides

Cappadocia's fascination reaches its height around sunrise when hot air balloons ascend into the sky, providing panoramic panoramas of the odd landscapes below. Drifting over fairy chimneys and valleys painted in red and orange is a once-in-a-lifetime adventure, leaving lasting memories.

Underground Cities

Explore the subterranean world of Cappadocia by visiting its underground settlements, such as Derinkuyu and Kaymakli. Carved into the soft volcanic rock, these communities served as refuge and protection during times of assault. Intricate tunnels, ventilation systems, and living rooms provide insight into the region's historical resilience.

Pamukkale

Pamukkale, meaning "cotton castle" in Turkish, is a natural wonder famous for its terraces of white mineral-rich hot springs. Nestled in southern Turkey, this resort invites guests to relax and delight in its remarkable geological formations.

Terraces and Thermal Pools

The beautiful white terraces of Pamukkale are generated by the rush of calcium-rich mineral springs rushing down the mountainside. Visitors may stroll barefoot on the terraces, enjoying the warm, mineral-rich waters that have been sought after for their claimed medicinal effects for generations.

Hierapolis Ancient City

Adjacent to Pamukkale, the ancient city of Hierapolis promises a trip back in time. Explore well-preserved ruins, including an amphitheater, agora, and necropolis. The location also contains the Martyrium of

Saint Philip, offering a dimension of historical and theological significance.

Nearby Attractions

Pamukkale serves as a gateway to other monuments such as the ancient city of Aphrodisias, known for its well-preserved stadium and Temple of Aphrodite. The travertine terraces of Karahayit, stained in tones of scarlet, are another adjacent treasure worth investigating.

In conclusion, Turkey's numerous sites provide a tapestry of experiences, from the historical richness of Istanbul to the strange landscapes of Cappadocia and the natural marvels of Pamukkale. Each area inspires exploration, generating a deep connection with the country's cultural past and natural beauty.

ACTIVITIES IN TURKEY

Turkey, with its rich cultural tapestry and different landscapes, provides a wealth of activities that appeal to a broad range of interests. From deep cultural encounters to exhilarating outdoor excursions, the activities offered in Turkey add to a well-rounded and unforgettable vacation experience.

Cultural Experiences

Traditional Turkish Bath

Embarking on a traditional Turkish bath, or "Hamam," is a cultural experience that immerses tourists in centuries-old customs of relaxation and regeneration. Istanbul, in particular, features antique hammams where one may relax in a calm setting embellished with beautiful tiles and marble. The ritual often comprises a series of steam, scrub, and massages, leaving participants with a strong sensation of physical and mental regeneration. The Turkish bath tradition is a pleasant blend of cleaning and cultural immersion, enabling tourists to engage with Turkey's ancient bathing rituals.

Whirling Dervish Performances

For those seeking a spiritual and artistic experience, witnessing a Whirling Dervish performance is a must. This captivating dance, known as the "Sema," is a type of devotion performed by the Mevlevi order of Sufism. The whirling dervishes, draped in flowing white robes, spin in a trance-like condition, signifying a journey toward spiritual enlightenment. Istanbul and Konya are renowned destinations where tourists may experience these mesmerizing performances. The mix of music, symbolism, and precise movements creates an ethereal ambiance, giving a unique glimpse into Turkey's magical legacy.

Outdoor Adventures

Hiking and Trekking

Turkey's varied geography is a playground for outdoor lovers, and hiking and trekking possibilities abound across the nation. One of the most renowned paths is the Lycian Way, a long-distance trekking route along the Mediterranean coastline, affording stunning vistas of the sea and ancient monuments. Cappadocia, with its distinctive scenery, boasts several routes that weave through valleys, fairy chimneys, and cave houses. Exploring Turkey's rich natural beauties on foot enables people to connect with the land, unearth hidden jewels, and observe the country's magnificent nature up close.

Water Sports

With its enormous coasts along the Mediterranean and Aegean Seas, Turkey is a sanctuary for water sports aficionados. Popular coastal resorts such as Bodrum, Fethiye, and Antalya offer a range of water sports, including snorkeling, scuba diving, and windsurfing. The crystal-clear waters, colorful marine life, and underwater caverns make these locations perfect for both beginners and seasoned water enthusiasts.

Turkey's seaside cities offer a great combination of leisure and excitement for those seeking an aquatic retreat.

Skiing in Winter

When winter covers the mountainous regions of Turkey, ski lovers travel to the country's best ski resorts. Uludağ, near Bursa, and Palandöken, near Erzurum, are recognized for their well-maintained slopes and sophisticated amenities. Skiing in Turkey provides a unique experience, with the ability to glide down snow-covered slopes against a backdrop of breathtaking surroundings. The winter sports season, normally ranging from December to March, draws locals and foreign tourists alike, creating a vibrant environment amid the snowy slopes.

In conclusion, Turkey's vast selection of activities means there's something for every tourist. Whether indulging in cultural traditions via a Turkish bath or whirling dervish performance, or pursuing outdoor experiences like hiking and skiing, the activities in Turkey add to a vacation experience that is both enlightening and invigorating.

FOOD AND DINING IN TURKEY

Exploring Turkish food is a gourmet trip that unveils a rich tapestry of flavors, textures, and cultural influences. From traditional delicacies to street cuisine pleasures, Turkey's culinary environment reflects its distinct history and regional differences, delivering a feast for the senses.

Turkish Cuisine

Must-Try Dishes

Turkish cuisine is a wonderful blend of Ottoman, Middle Eastern, Central Asian, and Balkan influences, resulting in a unique and tasty range of dishes. Some must-try foods include:

Kebabs: A fundamental component of Turkish cuisine, kebabs come in different forms, such as shish kebab (grilled meat skewers), döner kebab (spinning meat on a vertical spit), and iskender kebab (served over pita bread with tomato sauce and yogurt).

Mezes: These are tiny appetizers that demonstrate the range and freshness of Turkish ingredients. Popular mezes include hummus, dolma (stuffed grape leaves), and muhammara (red pepper and walnut spread).

Köfte: These are Turkish meatballs cooked with minced meat, often lamb or beef, coupled with spices and herbs. They are often grilled or fried and served with accompaniments like rice or bread.

Baklava: A sweet and flaky pastry consisting of layers of thin dough filled with chopped nuts and sweetened with honey or syrup. Baklava is a beautiful delicacy appreciated throughout Turkey.

Street Food Delights

Turkey's street food scene is a lively and crucial component of daily life, producing exquisite snacks that are both quick and pleasurable. Some street culinary items to sample include:

Simit: Often referred to as Turkish bagels, simit is a circular bread studded with sesame seeds, loved as a quick snack or breakfast item.

Balık Ekmek: A renowned street food in coastal locales, balık Ekmek consists of a grilled fish filet served in a bread roll with fresh vegetables and seasonings.

Midye Dolma: These are stuffed mussels packed with a delectable rice mixture, seasoned with herbs and spices. They are a popular street snack across coastal regions.

Kumpir: A baked potato stacked with many toppings like cheese, olives, corn, and sausage, kumpir is a hearty and customizable street food option.

Dining Etiquette and Customs

Turkish dining is a social and communal activity, reflecting the country's emphasis on hospitality. Understanding dining etiquette and customs gives a pleasant and pleasurable culinary adventure. Some important practices include:

Removing Shoes: When entering someone's home, it is common to remove your shoes as a mark of respect and cleanliness.

Sitting Arrangements: In traditional Turkish residences and restaurants, there is often a set sitting arrangement. The most respected guest is often positioned at the head of the table.

Sharing Food: Turkish meals typically involve shared dishes, encouraging a convivial dining experience. It's customary to give gifts and share meals with those around you.

Politeness: Expressing thanks for the supper, known as "afiyet olsun," is a polite way to thank the host or chef.

Recommended Restaurants by Region

Exploring Turkey's varied locales makes for a gourmet trip that runs from beach delights to strong Anatolian dinners. Some recommended restaurants by area include:

Istanbul: For a blend of Ottoman and modern Turkish cuisine, Mikla, located in Beyoglu, gives panoramic views and a superb dining experience. In the historic Sultanahmet district, visit Hamdi Restaurant for traditional dinners with a view of the Golden Horn.

Cappadocia: Set in a cave, Ürgüp's Ziggy Cafe & Restaurant gives a unique dining experience with a focus on local ingredients. For a taste of authentic Anatolian cuisine, Dibek Sofrası in Göreme is a popular alternative.

Bodrum: The Bodrum Peninsula is known for seafood, and Limon Restaurant in Yalıkavak is a seaside treasure delivering fresh catches and excellent views.

Alternatively, Bodrum Mantar Evi specializes in mushroom-based cuisine for a unique culinary experience.

Turkish cuisine is a celebration of flavors, textures, and culinary traditions passed down through the ages. Whether indulging in kebabs on the crowded streets or savoring a classy dining experience overlooking the Bosphorus, exploring Turkey's food and eating scene is an important aspect of the travel experience, offering a taste of the country's rich cultural past.

SHOPPING IN TURKEY

Turkey is a shopper's paradise, offering a diverse array of shopping experiences that appeal to all interests and inclinations. From traditional souvenirs exhibiting centuries-old craftsmanship to busy great bazaars and sophisticated shopping areas, Turkey urges guests to embark on a retail journey that embodies its rich cultural heritage and contemporary vigor.

Traditional Souvenirs

When exploring Turkey, traditional gifts serve as valuable memories that highlight the country's cultural distinctiveness. These artifacts reflect the exceptional craftsmanship and ingenuity profoundly engrained in Turkish heritage. Some common souvenirs to consider include:

Carpets & Kilims: Turkey is recognized for its amazing handmade carpets and kilims, having complicated patterns and vibrant colors. Each sculpture typically offers a tale and demonstrates a given region's unique style.

Ceramics & Tiles: Turkish pottery, particularly the legendary Iznik patterns, are timeless treasures. From finely painted plates to vibrant tiles, these objects capture the essence of Turkey's historical and cultural heritage.

Copperware: Turkish copperware, containing pots, pans, and decorative items, demonstrates the country's rich history of metal crafting. The Grand Bazaar in Istanbul is a terrific site to peruse a selection of well-made copper artifacts.

Evil Eye Talismans: A symbol of protection, the evil eye talisman is a common and essential recollection. These bright blue amulets are supposed to resist bad energy, are available in different forms, from jewelry to home décor.

Grand Bazaars and Markets

Turkey's beautiful bazaars and markets are immersive experiences that immerse guests into a world of vibrant colors, exotic aromas, and the hustle and bustle of trade. Navigating along the tiny passages, one may uncover an array of goods, from spices to textiles and everything in between. Key sites for a huge bazaar experience include:

Grand Bazaar, Istanbul: One of the world's oldest and largest covered markets, the Grand Bazaar in Istanbul is a labyrinth of businesses providing carpets, jewelry, spices, textiles, and more. Haggling is a typical practice here, adding to the colorful atmosphere.

Spice Bazaar, Istanbul: Located in the Eminönü area, the Spice Bazaar is a sensory feast. Aromatic spices, teas, chocolates, and Turkish delight inspire travelers to explore the colorful kiosks and savor the varied flavors of Turkey.

Kemeraltı market, Izmir: This historic market in Izmir is a treasure mine of antiques, textiles, and local crafts. It provides a more quiet setting compared to the Grand Bazaar in Istanbul, permitting people to meander along its aisles at their own time.

Modern Shopping Districts

In addition to its old markets, Turkey has modern retail districts that cater to contemporary interests and tastes. These districts contain upscale merchants, international brands, and cutting-edge designs. Notable modern retail zones include:

Nişantaşı, Istanbul: Often referred to as Istanbul's "Fifth Avenue," Nişantaşı is a sophisticated district famous for its high-end retail boutiques, designer stores, and trendy cafés. It attracted fashion connoisseurs and those seeking luxury brands.

Kanyon Mall, Istanbul: A sophisticated retail and leisure destination, Kanyon Mall in Istanbul features a mix of international and Turkish brands. Its inventive structure, with open-air rooms and cascading levels, delivers a unique shopping experience.

Bağdat Avenue, Istanbul: Stretching along the Asian side of Istanbul, Bağdat Avenue is a busy street studded with premium retailers, fashion outlets, and cafés. It's a popular spot for guests desiring a refined shopping and dining experience.

In conclusion, Turkey's varied shopping environment assures that every traveler finds something to suit their preferences, whether they're drawn to the traditional allure of enormous bazaars, the beauty of traditional trinkets, or the refined elegance of rich districts. Shopping in Turkey is not simply about obtaining items; it's a cultural and sensory experience that adds a level of richness to each visit.

HEALTH AND SAFETY

Ensuring health and safety are crucial problems for every traveler exploring a new environment. Turkey, with its different landscapes and rich cultural experiences, creates a pleasant environment for tourists. Understanding and prioritizing health and safety can lead to a smooth and happy journey.

Travel Insurance

Securing comprehensive travel insurance is an essential step in providing peace of mind during your vacation in Turkey. Travel insurance gives financial protection in case of unanticipated circumstances such as medical emergencies, trip cancellations, or lost luggage. Before coming to Turkey, it's suggested to review the coverage supplied by your insurance policy, ensuring it includes medical expenditures, evacuation coverage, and coverage for activities you want to engage in, such as adventure sports.

In the event of a medical emergency, having travel insurance allows access to professional care without the burden of exorbitant charges. It's recommended to carry a copy of your insurance policy details and emergency contact information with you at all times. Additionally, educate yourself on the method for filing claims and the contact details of the insurance provider's assistance service.

Health Precautions and Vaccinations

Prioritizing health precautions and vaccines is crucial when planning a trip to Turkey. While the country normally maintains excellent health standards, implementing preventive activities helps defend against probable health risks.

Before traveling, consult with a healthcare professional to ensure that routine immunizations, such as measles, mumps, rubella (MMR), and influenza, are up to date. Hepatitis A and B vaccines are also indicated for travelers, as well as typhoid and rabies vaccinations depending on the nature of your activities and the regions you plan to visit.

Turkey has different regions with varied temperatures, and during specific seasons, mosquito-borne illnesses such as the West Nile virus may represent a hazard. It's suggested to take steps, such as applying insect repellent and wearing long sleeves and pants, especially in rural or wooded regions.

Additionally, tap water in Turkey is normally safe in urban areas, however, it's suggested to use bottled or filtered water, particularly in more isolated locales. Ensuring food safety by eating well-cooked and well-managed meals further aids in a healthy holiday experience.

Emergency Services and Hospitals

Understanding the emergency services available and knowing the locations of hospitals and medical facilities is crucial for a traveler's well-being.

Turkey has a well-established emergency service system. The nationwide emergency hotline is 112, where qualified specialists may provide help and guide you to the relevant institutions. For non-emergency medical conditions, you may visit neighboring clinics or chat with the hotel staff for help.

In large cities like Istanbul, Ankara, and Izmir, you'll find well-equipped hospitals with English-speaking professionals. However, in more rural or remote regions, English proficiency may vary, therefore it's helpful to have a basic grasp of common medical terminology in Turkish or travel with a translation tool.

Pharmacies, referred to as "eczane" in Turkish, are plentiful, and pharmacists are often trained and may dispense over-the-counter medications. However, it's crucial to carry any prescription medications you may need, along with a copy of your prescription, in case of unplanned circumstances.

While Turkey is a safe area for holidaymakers, surprising situations occasionally occur. Staying aware of health precautions, having access to emergency services, and being prepared with travel insurance contribute to a safe and joyful vacation in this unique country.

Before visiting, it's necessary to check with official health agencies, such as the World Health Organization (WHO) or the Centers for Disease Control and Prevention (CDC), for the latest health and safety recommendations for your region.

CULTURAL INSIGHTS

Turkey, a bridge between East and West, boasts a complex cultural fabric fashioned by centuries of history, diverse influences, and a particular blend of traditions. Exploring the cultural insights of Turkey displays a dynamic and multifaceted nation that cordially welcomes travelers into its heritage.

Religion and Customs

Religious Diversity: Turkey is a primarily Muslim country, with Islam being the major religion. The majority of Turks practice Sunni Islam, and the country is recognized for its religious tolerance and diversity. In addition to Islam, there are also

Christian and Jewish communities, contributing to Turkey's tapestry of religious traditions.

Mosques and Islamic Architecture: Turkey is home to some of the most spectacular mosques and Islamic architecture in the world. The iconic Blue Mosque in Istanbul, with its magnificent tilework and soaring minarets, is a monument to Ottoman architecture. Hagia Sophia, once a Byzantine church and subsequently a mosque, is today a museum, presenting a unique blend of Christian and Islamic traditions.

Customs & Traditions: Hospitality is a key component of Turkish culture. Guests are treated with great respect, and providing food and drink is a common sign of goodwill. Removing shoes before entering someone's home is normal, and it's nice to return invitations.

The Turkish bath, or "Hamam," is a traditional washing activity that has been a part of Turkish culture for decades. It contains a succession of steam, cleansing, and massage, offering both bodily and spiritual regeneration.

Art and Architecture

Influence of Empires: Turkey's art and architecture exhibits the effects of numerous civilizations that have ruled the region, especially the Byzantine, Roman, and Ottoman empires. This combination of styles is seen in structures like the Hagia Sophia, where Christian mosaics blend with Islamic calligraphy.

Turkish Carpets and Textiles: Renowned globally, Turkish carpets are a reflection of the country's rich creative heritage. These handwoven masterpieces, decorated with vibrant colors and elegant patterns, usually express stories of the weavers' cultural and personal experiences. Turkish textiles, notably kilims and rugs, are coveted for their quality and craftsmanship.

Contemporary Art Scene: Turkey's contemporary art industry is growing, with Istanbul as its heart. Modern art galleries, such as Istanbul Modern, display the works of Turkish and international artists. Street art is progressively gaining prominence, bringing a new touch to urban landscapes.

Festivals and Celebrations

Eid al-Fitr and Ramadan: Eid al-Fitr, the festival honoring the completion of Ramadan, is one of the most prominent events in Turkey. Families gather together to enjoy celebration feasts, exchange gifts, and perform acts of goodwill. Ramadan, the month of fasting, is practiced with extraordinary zeal, and the evenings are highlighted by spectacular street celebrations.

Republic Day: On October 29th, Turkey observes Republic Day, marking the creation of the Republic of Turkey in 1923. Festivities include parades, concerts, and cultural events, with the largest festivities taking place in Ankara and Istanbul.

Şeker Bayramı (Candy Festival): Also known as Ramazan Bayramı, this festival is held after the completion of Ramadan. Families visit one another, have meals, and exchange "bayram" niceties. Traditional Turkish sweets, or "şeker," are a significant aspect of the festivities, hence the title "Candy Festival."

Appreciating these cultural insights boosts the holiday experience in Turkey. Whether seeing the grandeur of historic mosques, finding the active art scene, or participating in colorful events, travelers get a deeper grasp of the cultural mix that makes Turkey a fascinating destination. Respect for local customs, interaction with cultural traditions, and an open-minded approach combine with a profound and immersive knowledge of Turkey's rich past.

PRACTICAL INFORMATION

Navigating the practical portions of travel in Turkey improves the overall experience, helping travelers to seamlessly discover the country's varied landscapes, engage with its rich culture, and make the most of their holiday.

Local Transportation

Public Transportation: Turkey features a wide and efficient public transportation network, making it relatively straightforward to navigate between cities and between regions. In large cities like Istanbul, Ankara, and Izmir, you'll encounter well-developed metro, tram, and bus networks. Istanbul, in particular, boasts a sophisticated public transportation network that includes ferries and funiculars.

Intercity Travel: For traveling between cities, Turkey has a stable and inexpensive intercity bus network. Companies including Metro Turizm, Pamukkale Turizm, and Kamil Koç operate lines between big cities and villages. High-speed trains also connect vital areas, delivering a pleasant and time-efficient mode of travel.

Domestic Flights: Domestic flights are a sensible alternative for covering longer distances. Turkey has many domestic airports, and carriers like Turkish Airlines and Pegasus Airlines offer frequent flights connecting major cities. This is especially convenient for visiting sites like Cappadocia, where flights to Kayseri or Nevşehir allow simple access.

Taxis and Ride-sharing: Taxis are frequently available in urban areas and are generally affordable. Ensure that the taxi meter is employed or agree on a charge before initiating the journey. Ride-sharing services like Uber are also available in numerous regions, offering an additional option for rapid and transparent transportation.

Communication and Internet

Language: Turkish is the official language of Turkey, yet English is often used in tourist zones and big cities. In more rural or secluded regions, proficiency in English may vary; hence, having a basic acquaintance with common Turkish phrases could be useful.

SIM Cards with Mobile Internet: Upon landing, consider purchasing a local SIM card for your phone. Turkey has robust mobile networks, and prepaid SIM cards are available at airports, kiosks, and retailers around the country. This gives you local phone numbers and affordable mobile data for navigation and communication.

Internet Access: Most hotels, cafés, and restaurants feature free Wi-Fi, making it easier for travelers to stay connected. Additionally, public venues and attractions may feature Wi-Fi access, allowing you to share your experiences and keep in touch with friends and family.

Tipping and Bargaining Tips

Tipping Customs: Tipping is common in Turkey and is a means to offer appreciation for great service. In restaurants, leaving a tip of around 5-10% of the bill is typical. Additionally, it's normal to tip hotel personnel, tour guides, and drivers. While tipping is mandatory in certain situations, it's sometimes discretionary, and the amount could vary depending on the degree of service.

Bargaining Tips: Bargaining is a cultural behavior, mainly at markets and bazaars. When purchasing trinkets, textiles, or other products at markets like the Grand Bazaar, haggling is customary. manner it with a polite manner, and be prepared to negotiate the price. It's typical for the initial offered price to be more than the final agreed-upon one. Take your time, enjoy the process, and consider it a cultural exchange.

Cultural Sensitivity: While bargaining is part of the shopping experience, it's vital to do so wisely. Understand the cultural background and avoid overly harsh approaches. A friendly and tolerant approach is more likely to result in a successful and delightful engagement with local vendors.

In summary, practical information on local transportation, communication, and cultural standards prepares travelers to navigate Turkey with ease. Whether jumping on a tram in Istanbul, bartering for souvenirs, or remaining connected with mobile data, being informed of these practical difficulties contributes to a flawless and joyful visit to this unique country.

SUSTAINABLE TRAVEL

Embracing sustainable travel habits in Turkey not only enables tourists to experience the country's natural and cultural beauties but also helps to preserve its unique history. By adopting responsible tourist behavior, selecting eco-friendly housing, and connecting with local communities, visitors can have a positive effect while visiting this wonderful region.

Responsible Tourism Practices

Cultural Respect: Responsible tourism in Turkey starts with cultural sensitivity. Understanding and honoring local customs, traditions, and etiquette are crucial. This includes dressing modestly in holy areas, asking for permission before taking images of people, and respecting sacred places.

Minimize Environmental Impact: Reducing the environmental effect of travel is vital for sustainable tourism. Opt for eco-friendly transportation choices, such as public buses or shared rides, to limit carbon emissions. Follow the idea of "Leave No Trace" while visiting natural locations, ensuring you leave the environment as you found it.

Support Local Businesses: Choose to support local businesses, craftspeople, and markets. Purchasing souvenirs from local craftspeople not only protects the authenticity of your purchases but also directly helps the lives of the community. Dine in locally-owned restaurants that reflect the richness of Turkish cuisine and employ locally produced ingredients.

Wildlife Conservation: When partaking in activities involving animals, consider operators that stress ethical standards. Avoid activities that exploit or injure animals for amusement, and choose ethical wildlife tourist experiences that contribute to conservation efforts.

Eco-Friendly Accommodation

Green Certifications: Selecting eco-friendly hotel alternatives with recognized green certifications assures that your stay corresponds with sustainable standards. Look for hotels or guesthouses that have acquired certificates for energy efficiency, waste reduction, and water conservation.

Energy and Resource Conservation: Choose lodgings that employ energy-saving measures, such as utilizing renewable energy sources and energy-efficient equipment. Hotels using water-saving techniques and waste-reduction methods contribute to overall environmental sustainability.

Local and Sustainable Practices: Eco-friendly lodgings frequently incorporate local and sustainable techniques. This involves procuring locally produced items, increasing community participation, and establishing eco-conscious regulations. Staying at such businesses boosts the overall effect of your stay.

Community Engagement Opportunities

Cultural Immersion: Engage with local communities via immersive events that encourage cultural understanding. Participate in guided tours provided by local experts that share insights into the history, culture, and daily life of the town. Attend local events or festivals to celebrate and support cultural heritage.

Volunteering Opportunities: Explore volunteering possibilities that allow you to give back to the locations you visit. This could include engagement in local environmental initiatives, educational activities, or community development projects. Ensure that your volunteer efforts correspond with ethical and sustainable principles.

Responsible Travel Organizations: Connect with ethical travel organizations and community-based activities that foster sustainable development. Many NGOs in Turkey focus on safeguarding cultural heritage, aiding local economies, and advocating environmental conservation. By actively interacting in or supporting these projects, travelers may contribute to positive change.

In conclusion, sustainable travel habits in Turkey encompass a devotion to responsible tourism, a preference for eco-friendly accommodation, and an active connection with local communities. By adopting these ideals, travelers not only enhance their own experiences but also play a key role in sustaining the natural and cultural treasures of this spectacular area for millennia to come.

RESOURCES

Exploring Turkey may be substantially enhanced by tapping into numerous sites that supply crucial information, viewpoints, and resources for travelers. From useful websites and apps to recommended reading and navigation aids, these tools give a well-informed and delightful travel experience.

Useful Websites and Apps

Turkish Ministry of Culture and Tourism (goturkey.com): The official website of the Turkish Ministry of Culture and Tourism gives thorough information for travelers. From border procedures to cultural events, this site offers a trusted source for understanding the practical parts of your vacation.

Google Maps: Google Maps is an amazing tool for discovering Turkish cities and landscapes. Offering real-time directions, information on public transportation, and user evaluations of businesses, Google Maps simplifies the logistics of moving from one location to another.

Couchsurfing (couchsurfing.com): For those wishing for a more immersive and budget-friendly travel experience, Couchsurfing unites travelers with locals who give free housing. It's a terrific platform for cultural exchange and gaining insights from locals.

Culture Trip (theculturetrip.com): Culture Trip is a comprehensive travel website delivering articles, tips, and insights into Turkish culture, food, and sites. It's an excellent resource for scheduling your vacation and unearthing hidden gems.

Duolingo (duolingo.com): While many people in Turkey speak English, knowing a few simple Turkish phrases can drastically enhance your holiday experience. Duolingo is a user-friendly language learning tool that allows you to practice Turkish at your own pace.

Recommended Reading

"Istanbul: Memories and the City" by Orhan Pamuk: Nobel laureate Orhan Pamuk takes readers on a trip around Istanbul, offering a complex blend of personal biography and historical history. This book presents a complete perspective into the city's cultural layers.

"Birds Without Wings" by Louis de Bernières: Set against the backdrop of the collapse of the Ottoman Empire, this novel develops a tapestry of individuals and narratives in a tiny village in southern Anatolia. It portrays a devastating portrait of love, struggle, and cultural change.

"**A Fez of the Heart:** Travels around Turkey in Search of a Hat" by Jeremy Seal: Jeremy Seal's travelog takes readers on a delightful vacation throughout Turkey in quest of the legendary fez hat. Along the trip, he studies the country's history, culture, and the evolving dynamics of modern Turkey.

"**The Oracle of Stamboul**" **by Michael David Lukas:** This historical novel is set in Istanbul during the late Ottoman Empire. It tells the life of a brilliant young girl who becomes a genius in the area of politics and diplomacy.

Maps and Navigation Tools

Maps.me (maps.me): Maps.me is a user-friendly offline map application. Download complete maps of Turkey before your trip to explore without the need for an internet connection. It's particularly handy for exploring regions with poor connectivity.

HERE WeGo (here.com): HERE WeGo is a trusted navigation program that delivers precise directions, public transportation information, and offline maps. It's a great tool for traveling to both urban and rural sites in Turkey.

Turkish Road Atlas: For those going on road excursions or visiting rural locations, a genuine Turkish road map is a valuable resource. It offers detailed maps of transportation networks, and locations of interest, offering a thorough picture of the country's geography.

Google Earth: Google Earth allows you to digitally explore Turkey's landscapes and landmarks. It's a handy tool for picturing the terrain and obtaining a better knowledge of the country's different geography before and during your journey.

In conclusion, accessing these materials gives tourists the information and abilities essential to exploring Turkey with confidence. Whether seeking cultural insights, arranging itineraries, or finding your way through the colorful streets of Istanbul, these tools contribute to a well-rounded and fascinating travel experience.

CONCLUSION

Embarking on a vacation to Turkey is a compelling experience that mixes ancient history, vibrant culture, and magnificent nature. As you prepare for your holiday, consider these final advice and ideas to make the most of your visit to this magnificent country.

Final Tips and Recommendations

Embrace Cultural Sensitivity: Turkey's cultural diversity derives from its distinct history and traditions. Embrace cultural awareness by dressing modestly, respecting local customs, and engaging with the warmth and hospitality that Turks are famous for. A real interest in the local way of life will open doors to uncommon interactions.

Try Local Cuisine: Turkish cuisine is a highlight of each visit, delivering a delightful blend of flavors and textures. Don't miss the opportunity to enjoy local favorites such as kebabs, mezes, and baklava. Explore markets and street food sellers for a true gastronomic trip.

Explore Beyond the Tourist Hubs: While iconic destinations like Istanbul and Cappadocia are must-visits, consider going off the main route to explore lesser-known gems. Explore beach settlements, rural landscapes, and historical sights away from the tourist highlights for a more intimate and real experience.

Connect with Locals: Engaging with locals gives a broader knowledge of Turkey's culture and traditions. Whether via guided tours, cultural events, or chats in local cafés, contact with people lends a personal touch to your visit.

Stay Hydrated and Sun-Protected: Turkey has diverse temperatures, and keeping hydrated is crucial, especially in the warmer months. Carry a reusable water bottle, apply sunscreen, and wear a hat to protect yourself from the sun, particularly when exploring outdoor landmarks.

Be Cautious with Street Food:
While Turkish street food is fantastic, apply caution while deciding where to enjoy it. Opt for vendors with clean and hygienic surroundings, and examine popular spots where residents frequent to ensure the quality and safety of the meal.

Learn Basic Turkish Phrases:
While many Turks in tourist locations speak English, learning a few basic Turkish phrases can enhance your experience and endear you to locals. Simple greetings and expressions of appreciation go a long way in developing good ties.

Experience Traditional Arts: Turkey has a rich tradition of arts and crafts. Attend a traditional Turkish music or dance performance, explore local artisan workshops, or master the subtleties of Turkish calligraphy. These meetings reveal insights into the country's artistic heritage.

Respect Nature and Historical Sites: Whether walking in Cappadocia, exploring ancient ruins, or enjoying the natural wonders of Pamukkale, respect the environment and historical locations. Follow designated paths, refrain from littering, and be careful of the influence of your visit on these sensitive places.

Share Your Experience

As you conclude your journey around Turkey, consider sharing your experiences with others. Whether via travel blogs, social media, or personal experiences, your opinions inspire and educate other travelers. Share tips, recommendations, and amazing experiences to contribute to the collective knowledge of those planning their Turkish holiday.

Connect with the active travel community and share your photographs, anecdotes, and cultural experiences. Encourage sustainable and ethical travel practices, develop an understanding of Turkey's unique history, and encourage others to explore with respect and curiosity.

In sharing your tale, you not only chronicle your journey but also contribute to the wider tapestry of travel experiences. Your thoughts may motivate others to embark on their exploration of Turkey, providing a ripple effect of curiosity and respect for this lovely area.

In conclusion, as you say farewell to Turkey, take with you the memories of its landscapes, the echoes of its history, and the kindness of its people. May your experiences linger as a testament to the richness of Turkish culture, giving you a lifelong link to this exciting crossroads of civilizations.

Printed in Great Britain
by Amazon